RARE BIRD ALERT

STEVE MARTIN AND THE STEEP CANYON RANGERS

NEW SONGS FOR THE BANJO

BY STEVE MARTIN

& TRANSCRIBED BY TONY TRISCHKA

ISBN# 978-1-59773-327-4

HOMESPUN TAPES, LTD.
BOX 340, WOODSTOCK, NY 12498
WWW.HOMESPUN.COM

L SONGS WRITTEN BY STEVE MARTIN
(CEPT AS NOTED)
NGS COPYRIGHT © 2011 BY STEVE MARTIN

/DESIGN: G. CARR & SALLI RATTS GCARR.NET
SIC INSCRIPTION: ANDREW DuBROCK
VE MARTIN PHOTO BY SANDEE O. PHOTOGRAPHY

T0038194

TABLE OF CONTENTS

NOTES ON THE TUNINGS
By Steve Martin

As a reader of tabs and not of music, I can get very confused by alternate tunings. So here's my quick and dirty explanation of the various ones I use on *Rare Bird Alert*:

Open G: Nothing more to be said here.

Open D: I use this for "Rare Bird Alert" and "Go Away, Stop, Turn Around, Come Back." If you use D tuners, this is what they down-tune to. Almost. To put your banjo in open D, tune your third string down to match the fourth string at the fourth fret, then tune your second string to match your third string at the third fret. Then tune your fifth string up to match your first string at the seventh fret (or use a fifth string capo). Easy!

C Modal (or **Double C**): I use this tuning for "Yellow-Backed Fly," "More Bad Weather on the Way," and "The Great Remember." Starting in open G, tune your second string up a half step so it matches the third string at the fifth fret. Then lower the fourth string one full note, so when the fourth is fretted at the seventh fret, it matches the third string.

G tuning, alternate: Same as open G tuning, but with the fifth string tuned up to A. I use this tuning for "Best Love," "Northern Island," "You," and "Hide Behind a Rock."

INTRODUCTION

With *Rare Bird Alert*, Steve Martin and his barrage of banjos have once again stormed the parapet of the acoustic music world. Resistance is futile. Steve's last Homespun book, for *The Crow*, consisted of tunes old and new. This time, all tunes are newly minted, with the exception of "King Tut" (which goes back centuries).

Steve's creative faucet seems to be in a perpetual "on" position. After the release of *The Crow*, he wasn't sure he'd do another banjo album, but the tunes just kept coming. Those gems became *Rare Bird Alert*.

As of this writing, Steve's another five or so tunes into his next potential album, including one of his finest songs "Me and Paul Revere," which he and his musical cohorts, The Steep Canyon Rangers, performed at the Capitol Mall in Washington D.C. on the Fourth of July; just another example of Steve's banjo ambassadorship to the world.

It's interesting to note that many of the vocals on *Rare Bird Alert* started out as banjo tunes and with time became wonderfully lyricized. As with Steve's last tab book, some of the pieces are played in the three-finger style, while others were composed in the clawhammer mode. He's equally conversant in both arenas, a rare trait in a banjo player.

You'll notice that on *Rare Bird Alert* Steve continues to embrace a variety of tunings as he did on *The Crow*: D, Double C, G, G with the fifth string up to A, and so forth. This is a wonderful strategy for freshening up one's compositional outlook. Break the tyrannical bonds of open G tuning!

The music, as is always the case in Steve's world, is eminently playable. No double reverse back flips for the left hand, just accessible, highly original music. No mean feat. "Hide Behind a Rock" and "Northern Island" are two great examples.

Since *The Crow*, Steve's playing has deepened and expanded. Hitting the road with The Steep Canyon Rangers over the last couple of years has served to not only burnish his chops to a high and gleaming sheen, but also to introduce the banjo to its widest audience since the halcyon days of "Dueling Banjos." Backstage, when not doing a shake and howdy or nibbling at the deli platter, Steve can be seen practicing with the Rangers or working up a new tune on his own. No deep massages, leggy showgirls or peeled grapes. Steve's continuing passion for the banjo should serve as an inspiration to all players, student and professional alike.

—*Tony Trischka*

RARE BIRD ALERT

Tune your banjo to open D, bar the first three strings at the fifth fret, and you're off and running. For you clawhammer people it's not a difficult tune at all. In fact, once you get past learning the basics of the song, tuning your banjo to open D is probably the hardest part. If you play it with a band or in a jam, you can signal the pauses with an overt head nod, which can become more and more subtle as time goes on.

When I play this tune, I use mostly my second finger for melody. My thumb never drops. If you listen to the recording, I like to come in a hair early at the beginning of the B section, and I like to strum in odd places. Tony found ways to express these moments in the tablature. If I were you, and I am, I would learn it straight and then go about working on those subtleties.

—*Steve Martin*

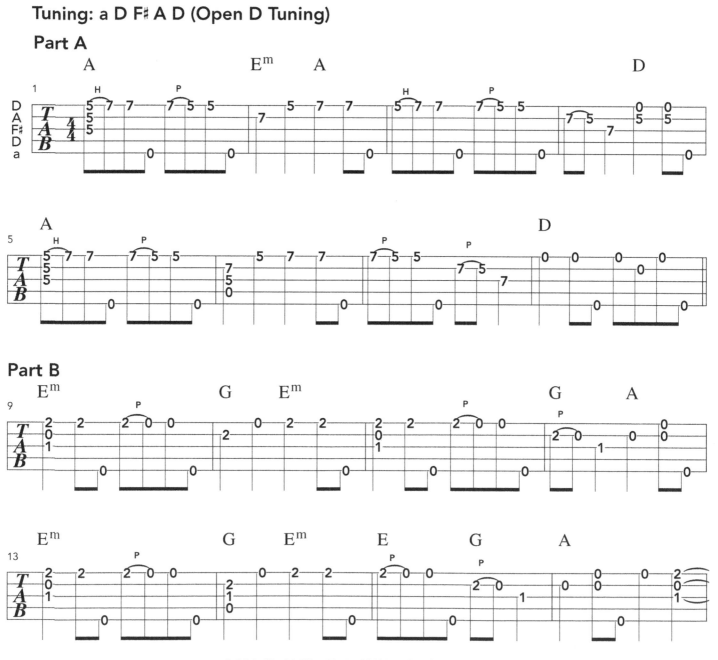

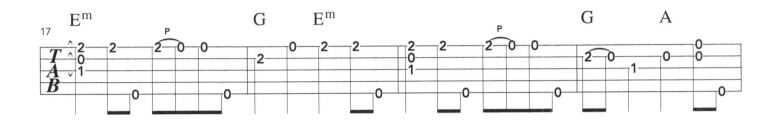

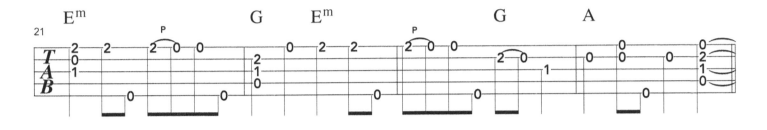

Part C

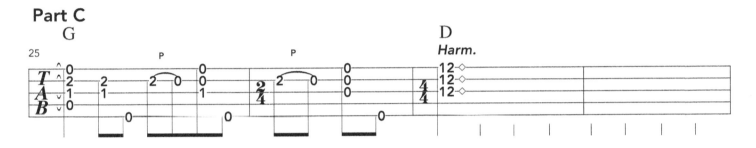

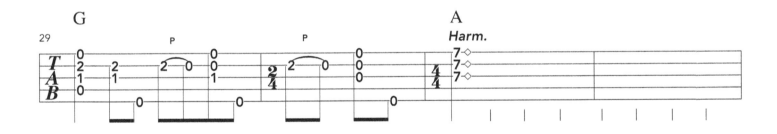

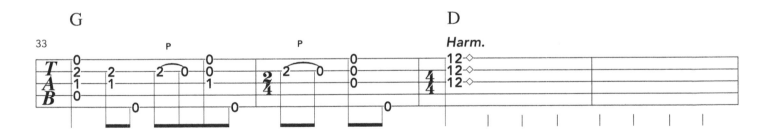

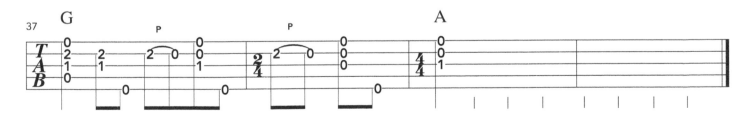

7

YELLOW-BACKED FLY

There are no secrets to this tune, simply tune to double-C, capo at the fifth fret (depending on the preferred key of the singer, of course), and play away. Just keep the bounce going. I sometimes think of the bounce of a very happy ball.

—*Steve Martin*

Key of F, Capo 5
Tuning: g C G C D (Double-C Tuning)
Verse

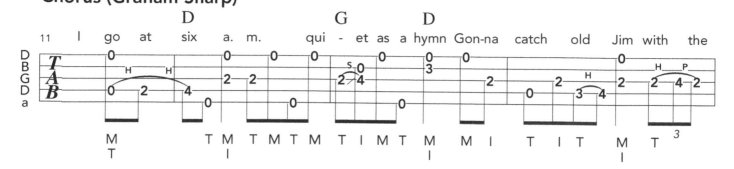

Key of F, Capo 3
Tuning: a D G B D (D Tuning)
Chorus (Graham Sharp)

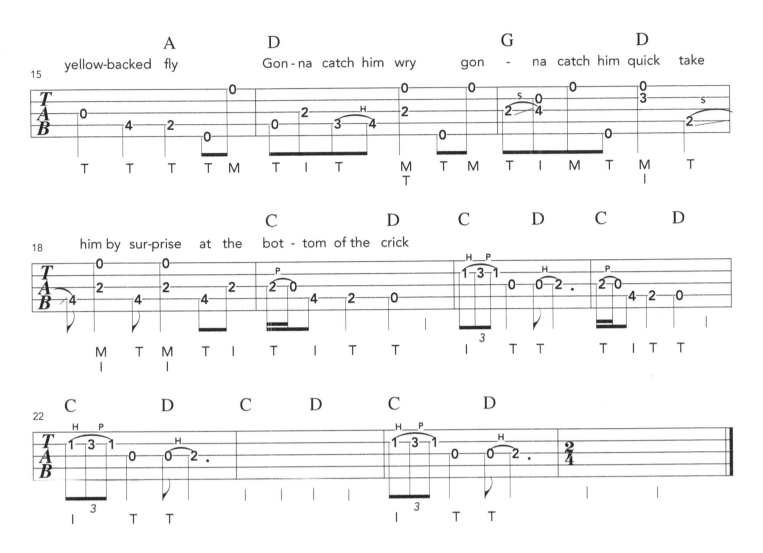

1. Carolina time, grab the fishing line
   Gonna get old Jim with the yellow-backed fly
   Bought it in a store, paid a little more
   Gonna catch that fish with the yellow-backed fly

2. Tried it last year with a lit firefly
   Laid it on the water with a perfect bullseye
   Jim made a splash, gone in a flash
   Beneath the water I heard him laugh

   Chorus
   I go at six a.m., quiet as a hymn
   Gonna catch old Jim with the yellow-backed fly
   Gonna catch him wry, gonna catch him quick
   Take him by surprise at the bottom of the crick

3. He lives beneath a rock, underneath the shade
   I will have him made with the yellow-backed fly
   Here I am at last, lying in the grass
   A quiet little cast with the yellow-backed fly

Chorus
Felt a little tug, old Jim had bit the bug
Then I let him run with the yellow-backed fly
Jumped up on the land, spit it in my hand
He said, "nice try with the yellow-backed fly"

4. Then he swam away, I gave him a farewell
   Now I'm going home with a story to tell
   I put the truck in gear, I'll be back next year
   Gonna make a fly with a hypnotizing eye

   Chorus (played twice)
   I go at six a.m., quiet as a hymn
   Gonna catch old Jim with the yellow-backed fly
   Twenty inches long, measured with a stick
   He's old Jim, but to me he's Moby Dick

9

BEST LOVE

This song actually started as an instrumental and I still enjoy playing it as one. However, if you want to employ a singer, I recommend getting Paul McCartney. I like the banjo backup on this to be rock-steady. This is a perfect song to practice with a metronome. A word of warning: the first time I ever worked with a metronome, I was convinced I had bought a faulty one. But after a few hours, I realized who was really at fault, and then the metronome became a good friend. Not one you'd want to take to dinner, however.

—*Steve Martin*

Key of E, Capo 2
Tuning: a D G B D (G Tuning, Alternate), capoed up to A
Verse

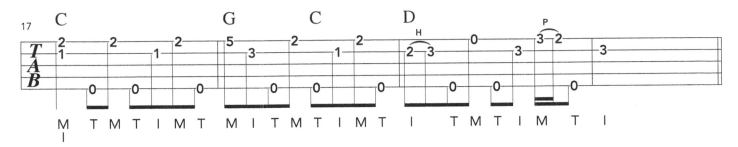

Chorus

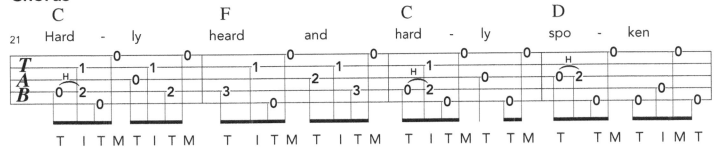

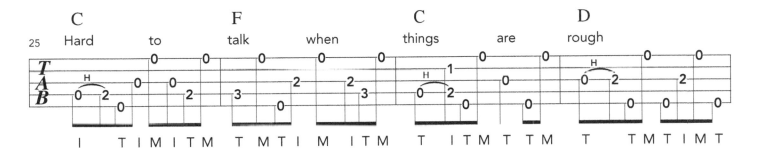

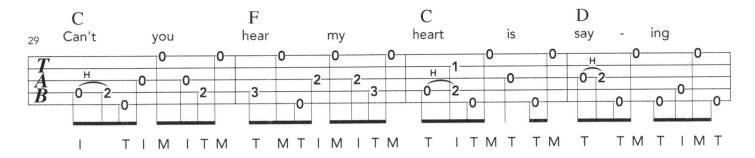

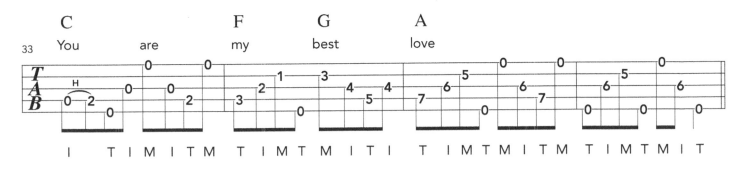

Verse (Break) Harmony—Graham Sharp

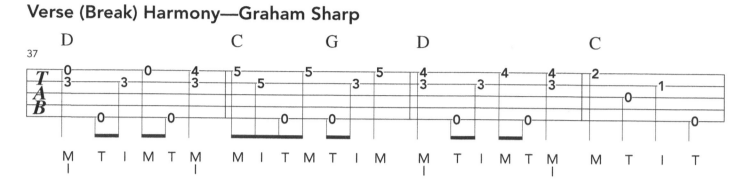

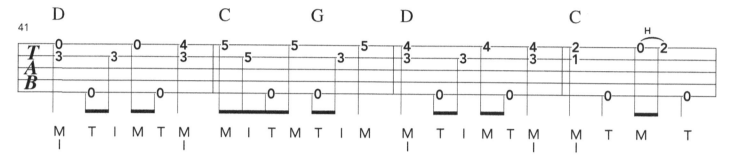

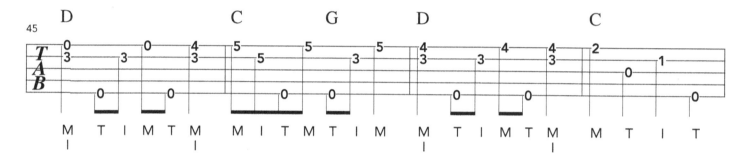

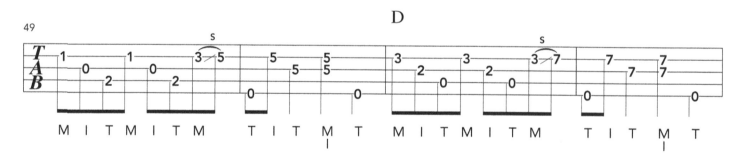

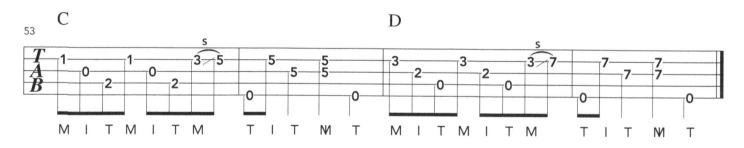

1. Things were nice in California
   Loved our trip out to the coast
   Did I say your mother phoned us?
   You are my best love

2. You look good in fancy dresses
   Wish we'd bought that one that day
   I even like your old ex-boyfriend
   You are my best love

   Chorus
   Hardly heard and hardly spoken
   Hard to talk when things are rough
   Can't you hear my heart is saying
   You are my best love?

3. Thanks for solving Friday's crossword
   Who knew Ivan was a czar?
   And for having patience with me
   You are my best love

   Chorus
   Silence is not my intention
   Hard to talk when things are rough
   Forgive me if I fail to mention
   You are my best love

   Repeat Verse 1
   Vocal ad-lib and fade

NORTHERN ISLAND

This can be played as fast as your speedy fingers can allow. Don't forget to tune the fifth string to A, or you'll think Tony has mis-tabbed the whole piece and played a dirty trick on you.

There's an odd little slide that takes place between measures four and five of Part A on the third string from the tenth fret to the fifth. I use my first finger (of my left hand) and it's nice in that it puts you in position to start the next phrase. But think of it as an invisible slide, as the right hand keeps playing the first, second and fifth string. It's just an element in the background, present while the right hand keeps picking.

I'm sure the lick that closes the end of every part A (measure 7) – sometimes it stays in the middle range of the neck and sometimes it ends down toward the headstock – can be played many different ways. This is the way I figured it out when I was writing the song, and sometimes I wish I'd worked it out differently, as it can be a finger-bender. You should feel free to work out your own, simpler method to reach these notes.

—*Steve Martin*

Tuning: a D G B D (G Tuning, Alternate)

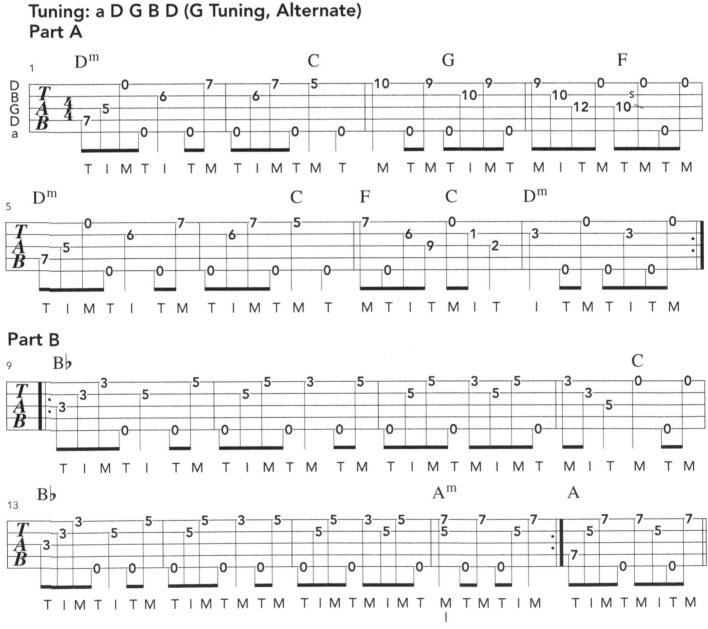

Part C

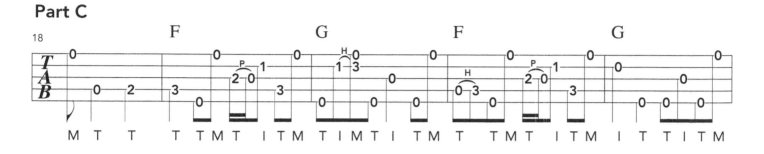

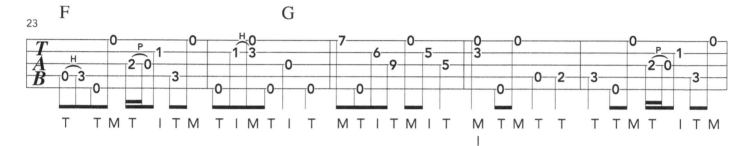

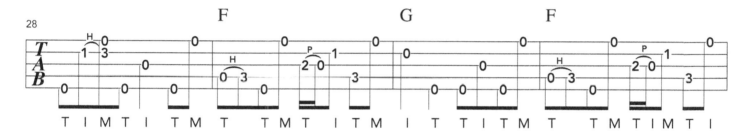

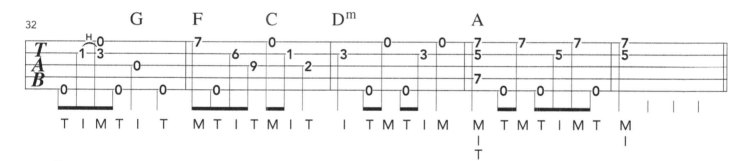

Part D

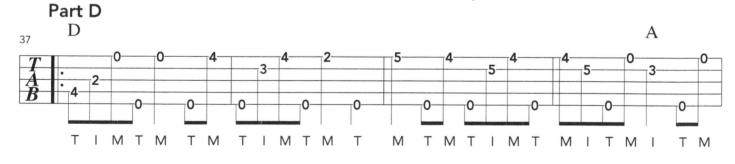

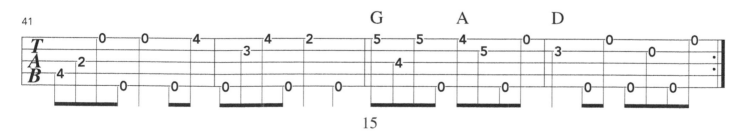

Part E

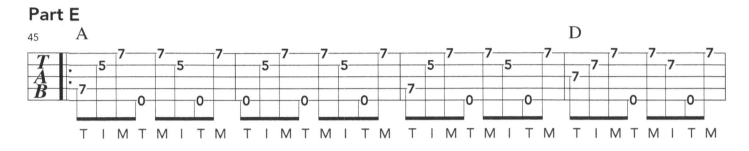

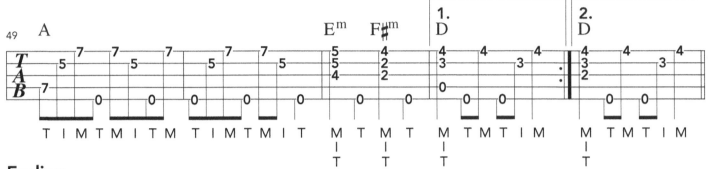

Ending

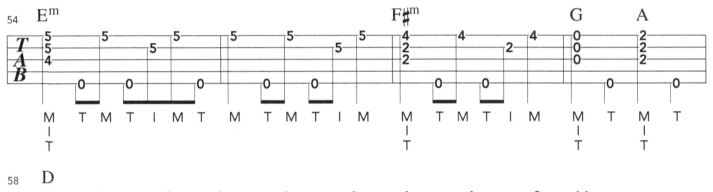

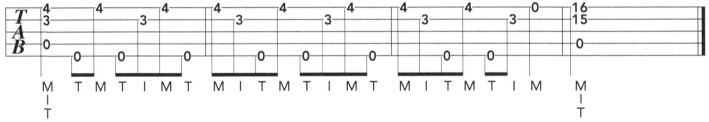

Part A Harmony (Graham Sharp)

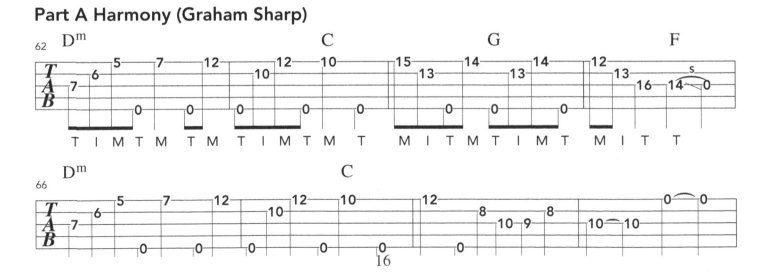

16

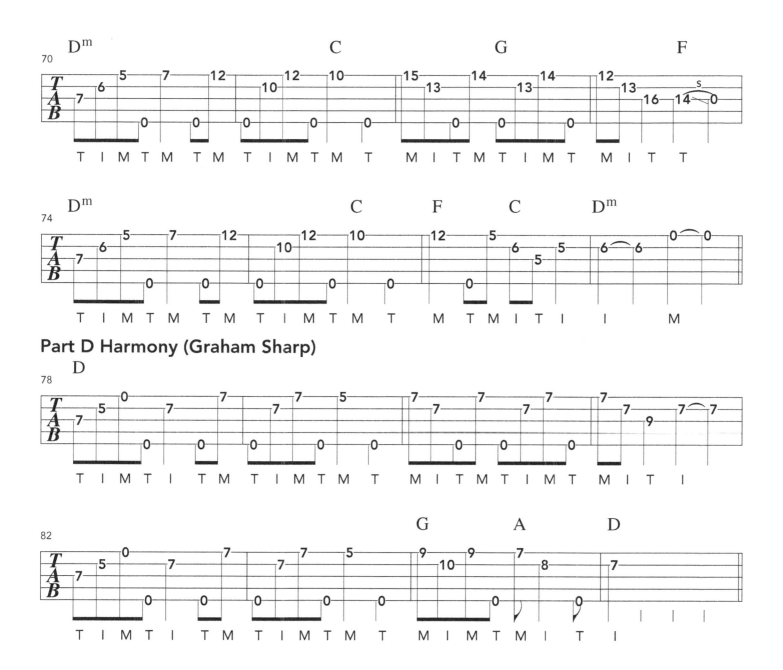

Part D Harmony (Graham Sharp)

GO AWAY, STOP, TURN AROUND, COME BACK

(Lyrics by Steve Martin. Music by Steve Martin, John Frazier, Woody Platt, Graham Sharp, Charles R. Humphrey III, and Nicky Sanders)

Tune your banjo to open D, and get ready to choke some strings; there's nothing too elaborate here. I've found in playing this on stage that the bending can be extreme or slight and it really doesn't matter. When Woody sings "I don't want to *bend* you," it's fun to give a little extra bend, but not enough to distract from the lyrics.

When the instrumental begins to repeat, in the D section, that's when the banjo must remain spot-on tempo-wise, especially if you're leading the way.

—*Steve Martin*

Key of E, Capo 2
Tuning: a D F♯ A D (Open D Tuning)
Verse

Published by LA Films Music (ASCAP), 53080 Publishing Co (ASCAP), French Broad Music (ASCAP),
Enchanted Barn Publishing (ASCAP), Lucks Dumpy Toad Publishing (ASCAP), and Fun and Play Music (ASCAP). All Rights Reserved.

Chorus

Instrumental

1. I don't want to lose you, though you might think I do
   I know I must confuse you, I swear I don't mean to
   When I say I love you, you know just what I mean
   My thoughts not quite in heaven, somewhere in between

   Chorus
   Go away, stop, turn around, come back
   Go away, stop, come back
   Go away, stop, turn around, come back
   Go away, stop, come back

2. I don't want to bend you, wrong to be that way
   Don't know where to send you, here or far away
   Let's just say it's over, time to move along
   Wait, it's Tuesday evening, our favorite show is on

   Repeat Chorus, two times
   Instrumental

3. When I say I love you, you know just what I mean
   My thoughts not quite in heaven, somewhere in between
   I don't want to lose you, though you might think I do
   I know I must confuse you, I swear I don't mean to

   Repeat Chorus
   Instrumental

JUBILATION DAY

This is really fun to play, and for once, we're in Open G! The audience seems to come alive with the traditional banjo kick-off, and the immediate Am chord, somehow, sounds, well, jubilant. I give it a little syncopation by sometimes leaving out a note in the first roll. It sounds like a delay, but it's not. I don't know how to explain it; listen hard to the record and you might hear it.

At the end of the phrase, before I start singing, I like the short slide down to the C chord (measures 6, 14, and 30). Make half a C chord one step up from normal (first finger on the second string at the second fret, third finger on the first string at the third fret), then play those two notes as you quickly slide it down to C position.

—Steve Martin

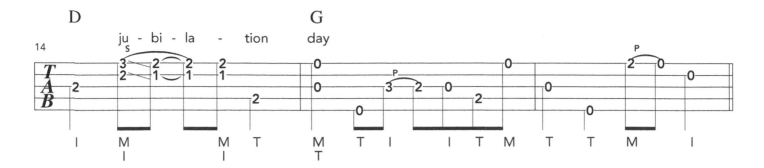

First Instrumental Break (after Verses 1 and 2)

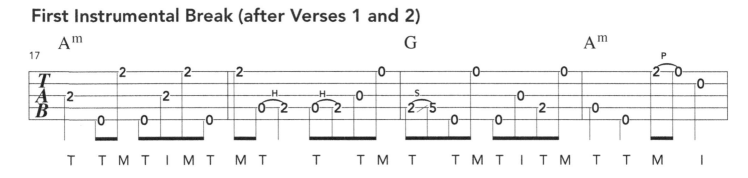

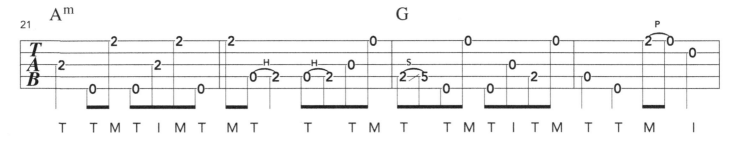

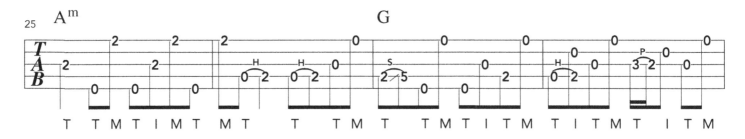

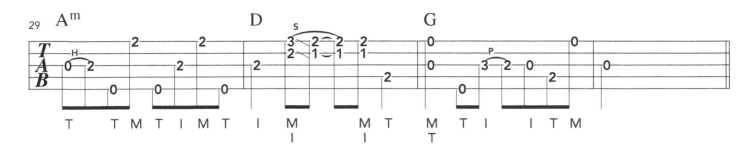

Second Instrumental Break (play both breaks in order after Verse 2)

1. I'm walking away like Dear Abby told me
   I'm walking away, my shrink gave his okay
   I'm walking away, the self-help book implored me
   I'm walking away, jubilation day

2. I'm walking away, my best friends all had warned me
   I'm walking away, even your mom said you were nuts
   In my dreams, you wear a red cape and a pitchfork
   I'm walking away, jubilation day

3. I'm walking away, let me get my things
   I'm walking away, where'd you hide my banjo strings?
   I'm walking away, I'll be over you by lunchtime
   I'm walking away, jubilation day

4. I'm walking away, let's always remember the good times
   I'm walking away, like when you were out of town
   I'm walking away, but the sex was great
   I'm walking away, at least that's what my best friend's brother said
   I'm walking away, you know, you're right, we should always stay in touch
   I'm walking away, this is your new email address, right?
   Cheating, psycho, dish-throwin' ho', dot nut
   Bye

MORE BAD WEATHER ON THE WAY

This is a tricky clawhammer tune that I love to play. It's tricky only because of the change of keys that occurs mid-tune, but since you bought the book, you're entitled to its dark, magical secret.

With the banjo un-capoed, tune the banjo to double C. Then, take a Shubb capo, the kind with the lever that pops the capo on and off, and clamp it at the fifth fret, and put your fifth string under a rail spike five frets up. You have to be extremely careful to lay the capo just right over the fifth frets, so as to require *as little retuning as possible.* A little practice will tell you just the right pressure that the capo should have and at what distance the capo should be behind the frets (usually, as near to, or even on top of the frets is best).

Then, learn the song. In the A section, the melody is played by the first finger on the 4th and 3rd strings and the thumb drops down occasionally to the 4th string to give a snap or off-tempo syncopation.

When it's time to change keys, you simply strum along, then, at the appropriate moment, snap off the Shubb and have it land quietly on a pillow, or sofa, or in a beehive hairdo. I've found that the 5th string can stay capoed and it sounds fine, especially if underplayed with a light touch.

—*Steve Martin*

Capo 5 (Key of F), Pop Capo Off for Key Change (Key of C)
Tuning: g C G C D (Double-C Tuning)
Part A

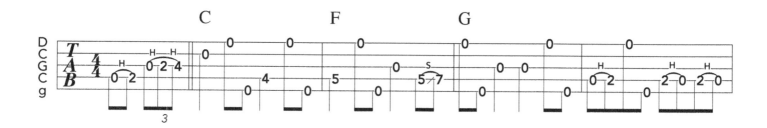

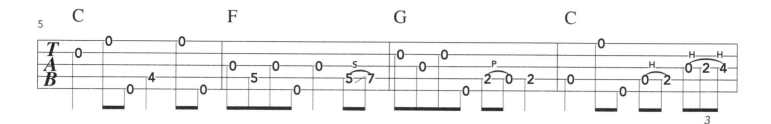

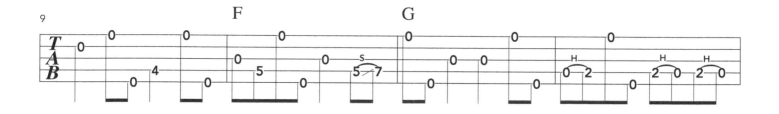

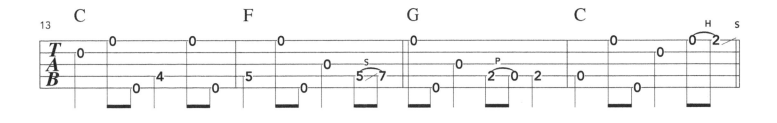

Part B

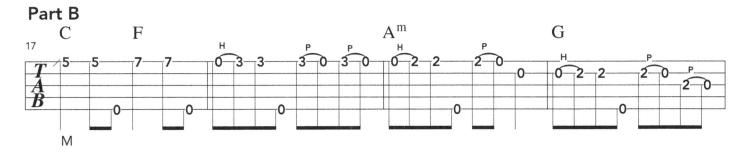

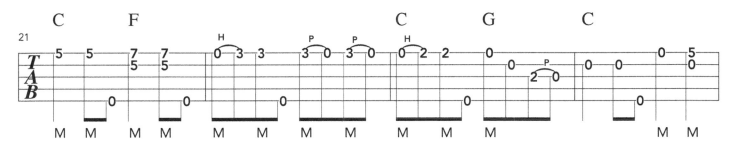

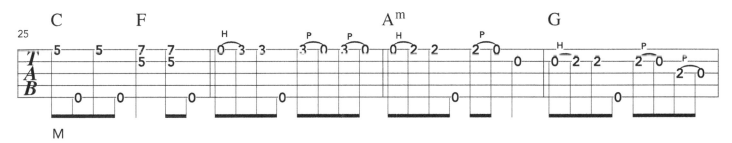

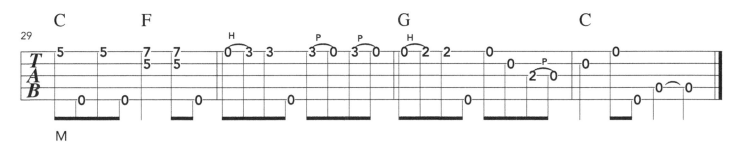

YOU

For this song, I tuned my hyper-sensitive arch-top Gibson Florentine (my first collectible banjo) down to D, put on heavy strings, hoping that every slide and finger squeak could be heard on the recording. To begin, it's just solo banjo playing chords, some of which are hammered-on just ahead of the beat. Also, sometimes I slide the entire chord down five frets or so just as I lift off on the chord change, and let the listener know it's being slid, too. If you play it with a singer, you'll find that sometimes you'll have to mute the strings with a left hand finger so the wrong chord doesn't ring through when you want to drop out.

—*Steve Martin*

Key of D

Tuning: a D G B D (G Tuning, Alternate), tuned down 2½ steps (e A D F♯ A)

Verses 1, 2 and 4

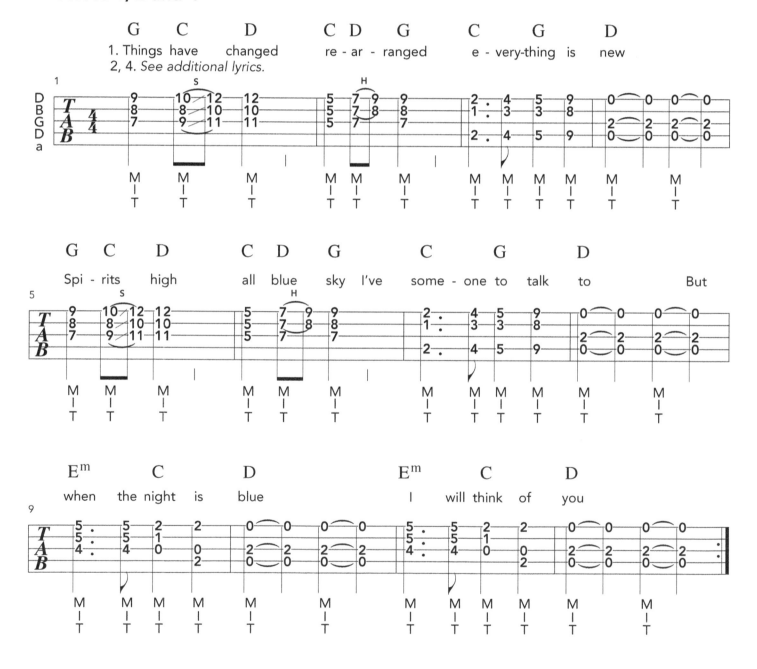

Instrumental Break (after Verses 2 and 3)

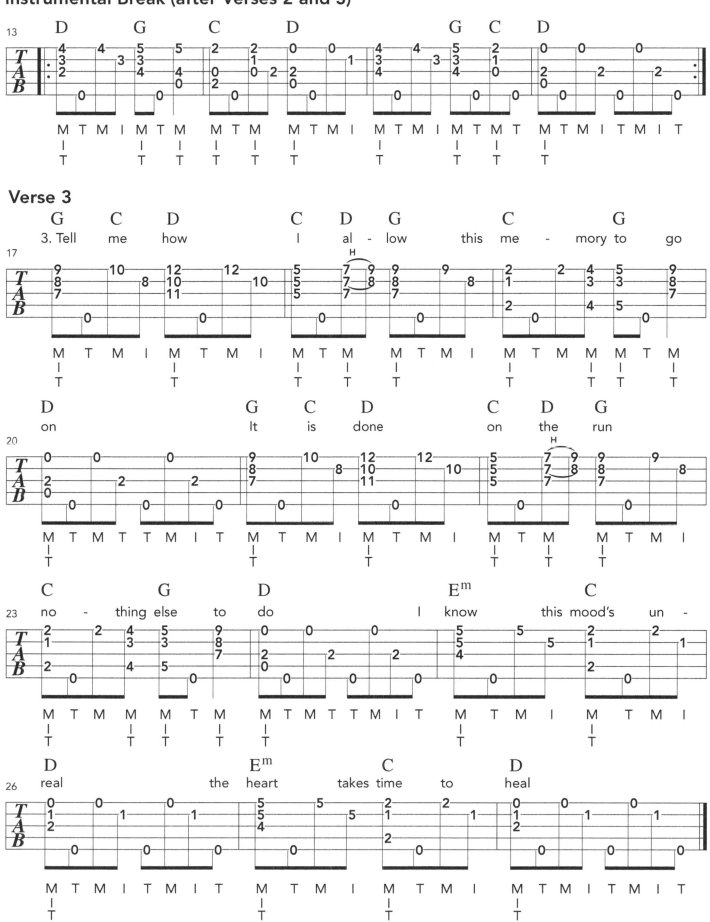

Verse 3

1. Things have changed, rearranged, everything is new
   Spirits high, all blue sky, I've someone to talk to
   But when the night is blue, I will think of you

2. Someone who loves me, too, after you withdrew
   Kinder ways, better days, words exchanged are true
   But winter settles in, thoughts of you begin

3. Tell me how I allow this memory to go on
   It is done on the run, nothing else to do
   I know this mood's unreal, the heart takes time to heal

4. Time goes on, days are long, summer's gone, you
   Saturday, sadder days, silence plays, you
   And when the night is blue, I still think of you

THE GREAT REMEMBER

This is a clawhammer tune that will test your ability to *leave things out.* The banjo is barely brushed, the third string is gently bent in measure seven of Part A (not every time, though, pick and choose as you go along whether to bend, or slide up to the tenth fret), and notes are softly, though clearly, struck. Sometimes when I play this, I realize I'm brushing the first string only (with my second finger or third finger). All those missing tones are being replaced with *air.*

At the end of the C section (measures 40 through 42), there's a string of descending single notes. It took me a while to discover that I was playing only the note itself with my first finger, while my thumb lightly struck the head in between. If you want to accomplish this, don't think about your thumb and first finger, just pull your right hand away from the banjo, *as though you were brushing and hitting the fifth string, but not reaching them.* The sound will take care of itself. In these three measures the tablature indicates that you hit the fifth string twice in a row. Actually, the first fifth string will be where you hit the head and the second fifth string will be activated as you come off the head. This technique continues through the first two measures of Part A'. In my stage show with the Steep Canyon Rangers, when I play these solo notes, I've noticed that is when the audience becomes quietest.

—*Steve Martin*

Tuning: g C G C D (Double-C Tuning)

Part A

Part B

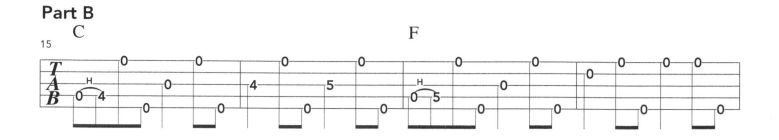

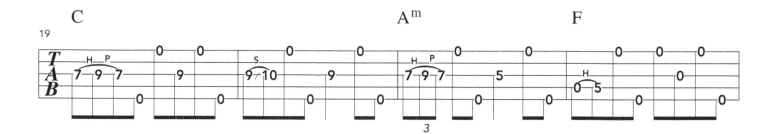

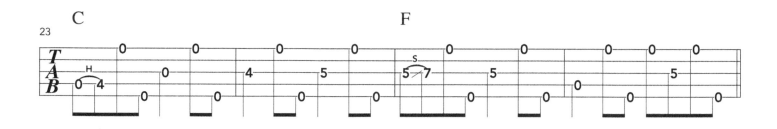

Part C

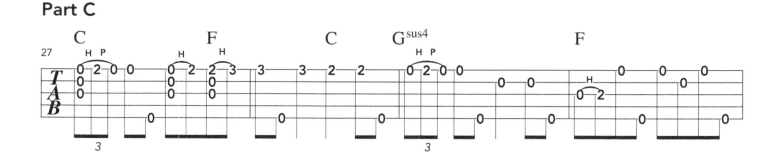

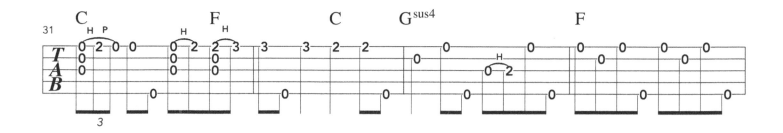

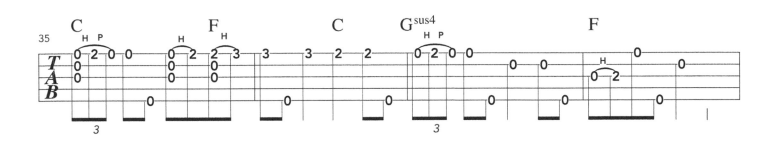

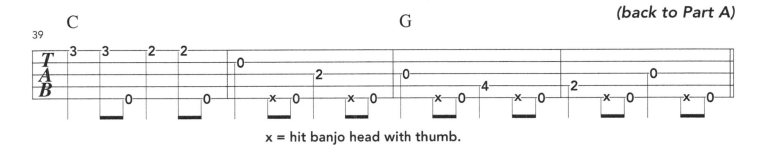

x = hit banjo head with thumb.

Part A' *(substitute for first time through Part A upon return to Part A)*

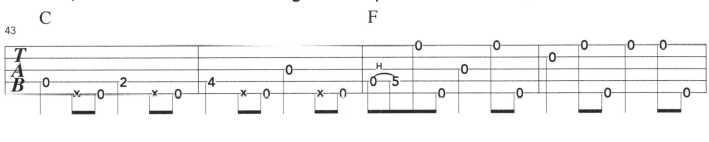

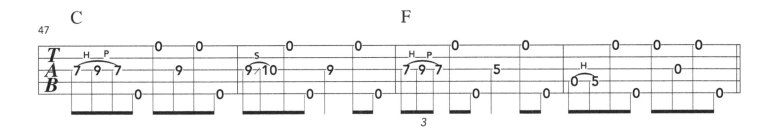

WOMEN LIKE TO SLOW DANCE

(By Steve Martin, Charles R. Humphrey III, and Phillip Barker)

Straight-ahead bluegrass. My break is tabbed out, but on this tune it's Graham Sharp who took the banjo flag and carried it over the finish line.

—*Steve Martin*

Tuning: g D G B D (Open G Tuning)

Intro

Verse

1. Find the girl___ you're think-ing a-bout___ take a chance___ and take her out___
2. *See additional lyrics.*

On the town___ to cut a rug___ if she's the one___ you real-ly love___

If you want___ that night to last___ don't you try___ and move___ too fast

Bet-ter not___ jump the gun___ just re-lax___ and have___ some fun

Chorus

Wo-men like___ to slow dance___ they like it for the ro - mance___

If you want to have a chance___ you got - ta learn to slow___ dance

Steve's Solo

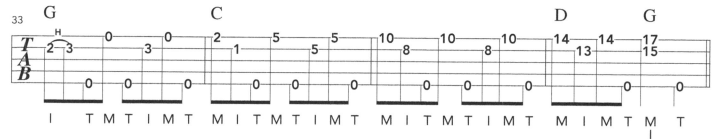

Graham Sharp's Solo

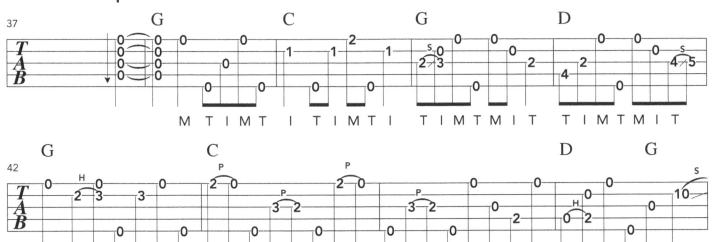

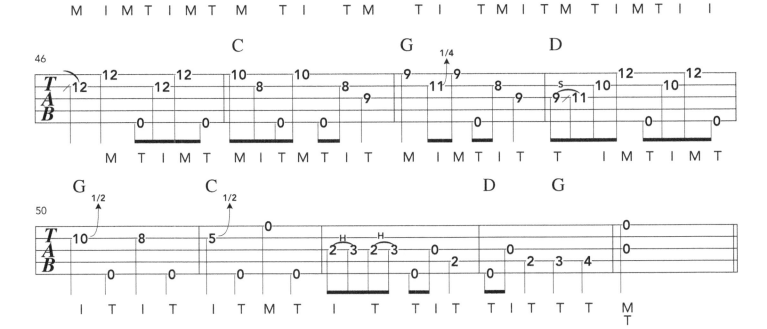

1. Find the girl you're thinking about, take a chance and take her out
   On the town to cut a rug, if she's the one you really love
   If you want that night to last, don't you try and move too fast
   Better not jump the gun, just relax and have some fun

   Chorus
   Women like to slow dance, they like it for the romance
   If you want to have a chance, you gotta learn to slow dance

2. Take the time and learn to waltz, she'll overlook your other faults
   There's magic in three-quarter time, pace yourself and you'll be fine
   Slow and steady wins the race, and puts a smile there on her face
   She'll be satisfied and pleased, every time, guaranteed

   Repeat Chorus
   Women like to slow dance
   (They like it, they like it, they really, really like it
   Hey, I like it too! It's romantic)
   They like it for the romance

   Repeat Chorus, two times
   Women like to slow…
   (Come on, baby! Now let's do a fast dance)

HIDE BEHIND A ROCK

This song is intended to be a fiddle and banjo tune, but I found it hard to play both at the same time. Best to get a fiddler to play along.

Once you get the basic moves of the song down, you can concentrate on the one or two subtleties which Tony expressed well in the tablature. The most puzzling is the unstruck hammer-on between measures 2 and 3 and measures 6 and 7. It's a bit ghostly and I don't hammer down hard. The right hand has moved on to other business, but the note, 3rd string, 5th fret, is hammered down to the 7th fret, in tempo, unplayed by the right hand.

—*Steve Martin*

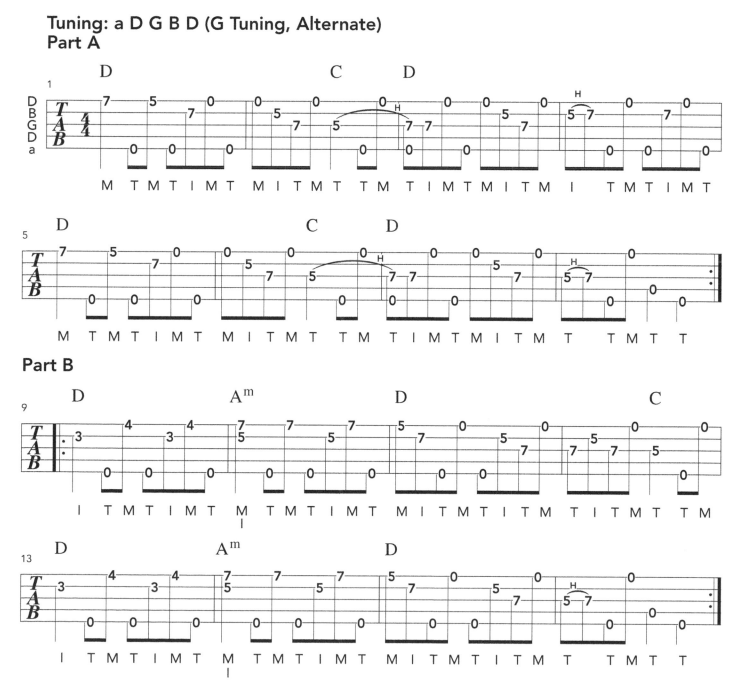

Part C

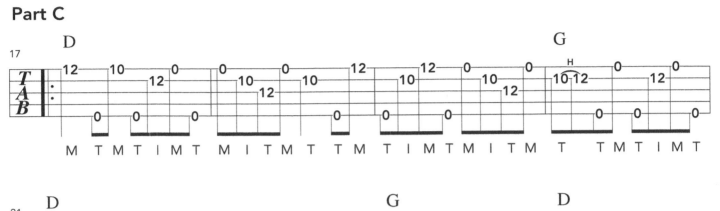

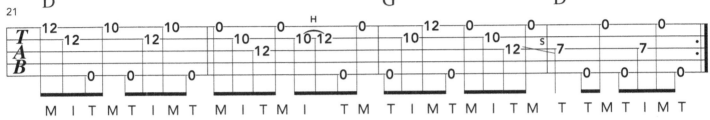

ATHIESTS DON'T HAVE NO SONGS

(Lyrics by Steve Martin. Music by Steve Martin, Woody Platt, and Graham Sharp)

Because gospel is so intrinsic to bluegrass music, I thought there should be at least one gospel song that represents those who might not be religiously inclined, even though I think of this song as quite neutral. It always gets a great response in our live shows, but I'm never clear just what it is that the audience is reacting to. The humor, I suppose, which speaks well of whatever side of the religious question they might be on.

I had written the lyrics, slowly and steadily—it wasn't easy to find a rhyme for "godless existentialism"—but I had no idea how to write a gospel melody to set it to. Woody and Graham took the challenge and showed up one day with the music entirely composed, and I loved it instantly. It remains a highlight of our live show. I could never hit the high note if it were a serious song, but because it's a comedy, and I feel I'm playing a character, I can do it.

—*Steve Martin*

1. Christians have their hymns in pages (hymns in pages)
   Hava Nagila's for the Jews
   Baptists have the Rock of Ages (Rock of Ages)
   Atheists just sing the blues

2. Romantics play Clair de Lune (Clair de Lune)
   Born-Agains sing "He is risen"
   But no one ever wrote a tune (wrote a tune)
   For godless existentialism

   Chorus
   For atheists there's no good news, they'll never sing a song of faith
   In their songs they have a rule: the "he" is always lowercase
   The "he" is always lowercase

3. Some folks sing a Bach cantata (Bach cantata)
   Lutherans get Christmas trees
   Atheists songs add up to nada (up to nada)
   But they do have Sundays free (have Sundays free)

4. Pentecostals sing to heaven (sing to heaven)
   Coptics had the Book of Scrolls
   Numerologists count, they count to seven (count to seven)
   Atheists have rock and roll

   Repeat Chorus
   Atheists don't have no songs

   (sing up a whole step)
5. Christians have their hymns and pages (hymns and pages)
   Hava Nagila's for the Jews
   Baptists have the Rock of Ages (Rock of Ages)
   Atheists just sing the blues

   Chorus
   Catholics dress up for Mass and listen to Gregorian chants
   Atheists just take a pass, watch football in their underpants
   Watch football in their underpants
   Atheists don't have no songs (don't have no songs)

KING TUT

Why would you want to play this? Well, if you've read this far, I'll assume there must be a very good reason, so I'll continue. Since the song is all in fun, play it for fun. It worked for me.

It's Graham Sharp who's got the good chops on this one, since I'm mostly singing it onstage. Graham made up his break; I got my licks directly from the hieroglyphs of King Tut's Tomb.

—Steve Martin

Key of A, Capo 2
Tuning: g D G B D (Open G Tuning)
Intro (Graham)

see   Peo - ple stand in line   to   see the boy   king

(King   Tut) ___   (King

C   **G**

How'd you   get so   funk - y

Tut)   (funk - y Tut)

D

Did you   do the monk - ey   Born in A - ri - zo - na   moved __

C   **G**   **D**

__ to Ba - by - lo - nia King   Tut

Steve's Solo

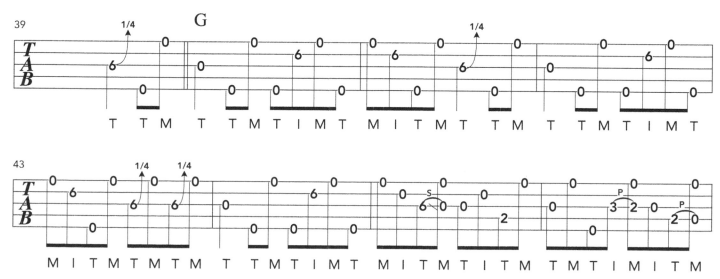

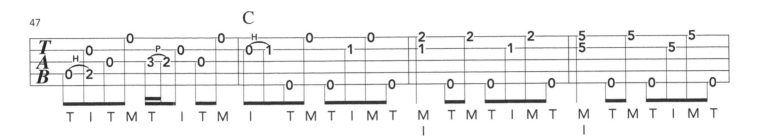

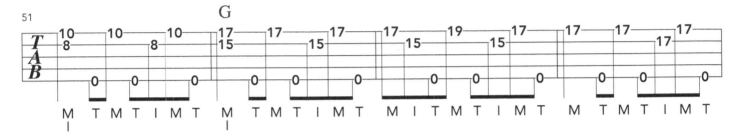

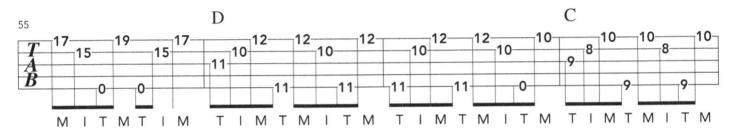

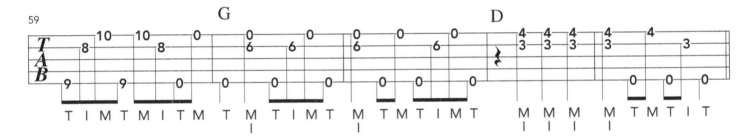

Graham Sharp's Solo

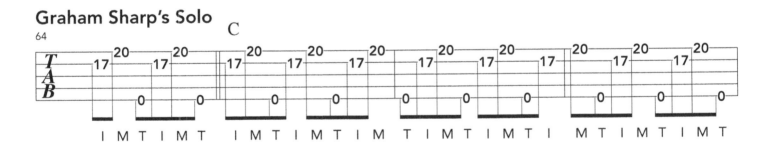

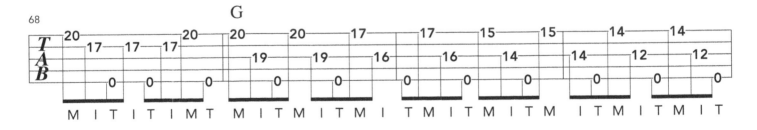

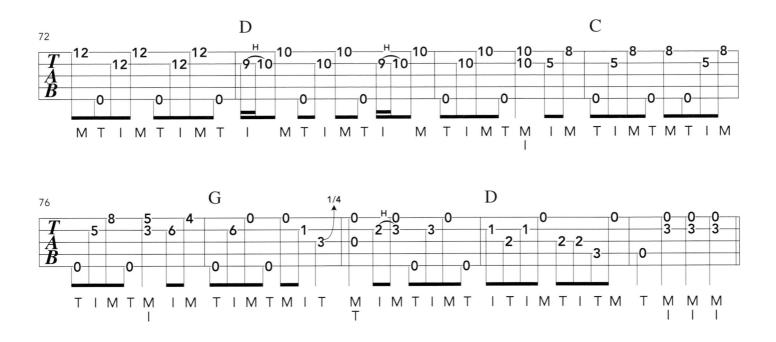

(King Tut, King Tut)

1. Now, when he was a young boy, he never thought he'd see (King Tut)
    People stand in line to see the boy king (King Tut)
    How'd you get so funky? (funky Tut)
    Did you do the monkey?
    Born in Arizona, moved to Babylonia, King Tut

2. Now, if I'd known they'd line up just to see him
    I'd taken all my money and bought me a museum (King Tut)
    Buried with a donkey (funky Tut)
    He's my favorite honky
    Born in Arizona, moved to Babylonia, King Tut

3. (Tut, Tut) Dancing by the Nile (Tut, Tut)
    (Tut, Tut) The ladies loved his style (Tut, Tut)
    (Tut, Tut) Rockin' for a mile (Tut, Tut)
    (Tut, Tut) He ate a crocodile (Tut, Tut)
    (Ooh) He gave his life for tourism (Tut, Tut)

4. Now when I die, now I don't think I'm a nut
    Don't want no fancy funeral, just one like old King Tut (King Tut)
    He could have won a Grammy (King Tut)
    His sister was his mommy
    Born in Arizona, moved to Babylonia
    He was born in Arizona, got a condo made of stone-a, King Tut

Transcription: Tony Trischka

Music Engraving and Layout: Andrew DuBrock